Stealing Home

HAGIOS
PRESS

Stealing Home

Dwayne Brenna

Hagios Press
Box 33024 Cathedral po
Regina sk s4t 7x2
www.hagiospress.com

Copyright © 2013 Dwayne Brenna

All rights reserved. No part of this publication may be reproduced, stored in a retrieval system, or transmitted in any form or by any means without the prior written permission of the publisher or by licensed agreement with Access: The Canadian Copyright Licensing Agency. Exceptions will be made in the case of a reviewer, who may quote brief passages in a review to print in a magazine or newspaper, broadcast on radio or television, or post on the Internet.

Library and Archives Canada Cataloguing in Publication

Brenna, Dwayne, 1955-
   Stealing home : baseball poems / Dwayne Brenna.

ISBN 978-1-926710-21-1

   I. Title.

PS8553.R3822S74 2013   C811'.6   C2012-905471-2

Edited by Robert Currie
Designed and typset by Donald Ward
Cover art: *The Player*, Memory Roth
Cover design by Tania Wolk, Go Giraffe Go Inc.
Set in Minion Pro and Courier New

The publishers gratefully acknowledge the assistance of the Saskatchewan Arts Board, The Canada Council for the Arts, and the Creative Industry Growth and Sustainability program, made possible through funding provided to the Saskatchewan Arts Board by the Government of Saskatchewan through the Ministry of Tourism, Parks, Culture, and Sport.

To the Naicam Vikings, the Lake Lenore Lakers, the Saskatoon Outlaws, the Saskatoon Royals, the Regina Jets, the TBarC, the Yanks, the Pioneers, the Sask Sportsmen, Sask-Alta, the Riverhurst Thumpers, the Red Deer Playboys, the Saskatoon Cardinals, and the kids and coaches at Inner City Baseball

> and now that I think of it, to my brother and my dad, both southpaws to be reckoned with in their day

> "The hardest thing to do is to walk away from your teammates and what they've meant to you over the years."
> — Jason Varitek, at his retirement in 2012

Contents

1. Field Days

Ebbets Field   12
Candlestick Park, San Francisco, 1984   13
The Big O, Montreal, 1988   14
Cleveland Stadium, circa 1990   15
Town Mead Leisure Park, Essex, 1993   16
Shea Stadium, New York City, 2005   17
House Made Of Pollen: Hohokam Stadium, Phoenix, 2008   19
Cairns Field, Saskatoon, 2010   20

2. Home Plate

You're Gonna Like This Game   23
A Boy Looks at his Reflection in the Window   24
Car Ride   25
Cheats   26
Beer Gardens   27
Alger   28
Apology (Or Close As It Gets)   30
Sports Day   31
No Fun   32
Bunt Defence   33
Voodoo   34
Evening of the Tournament   36
Fan   38
Canadian Oldtimers' Championship, Red Deer, 2007   39
Didn't Look That Awkward   40
To Mrs. Towny Townsend, Chesapeake, Virginia   41
Blue Team   42
Funeral   43
Double Play   44
Ya Gotta Want the Ball   45

Umpiring 46
Coaching Clinic 47
WinnWell 48
Fastball 51
Chatter 52
Curveball 53
Knuckleball 54
Split Finger 55
Circle Change 56
Catcher 57
Base Ball 58
Seams/Seems 59
The Origins of Baseball 60
The Tao of Baseball 61

4. The Mound of Venus

Ladies' Softball 65
How to Talk to Girls 66
Fat Girls in Yorkton 68
Physiotherapy 71
Lonely Hearts 72
Cantankerous Baseball Card Collector Seeks
　　Large-Breasted Statistician 73
Groupie Wanted 74
Sarandon 75
Woody Allen 76
The Mound of Venus 77

5. Bambino and the Boys

Autograph   81
Pointing to the Stands   82
The Babe on Film   83
The House that Ruth Built   84
Footnote   85
Christy   86
Mickey and the Stripper   87
1951—Some Photographs   88
Symmetry   90
Casey   91
Stats and the Great Players   92
Drysdale   93
Scully   94
Baseball's Music   95
Wonderboy   96
Ellis   97
Interview with Jim Fanning   98
Mobile, Alabama   99
Satch's Blues   101
Stealing Home   102

Acknowledgements   103

1. Field Days

"If this is a ballpark, I'm a Chinese aviator."
— Billy Martin on the new Metrodome

Ruts

What vivid anger drove him to this place
to rail and vent against all innocence?
Did a coach in Little League chastise him for a missed pop fly?
A father shout at him for striking out?
Was he bullied by some bigger kid who wanted shortstop to himself?
Maybe he was sick of winter. That can happen in Saskatchewan.
We're all as mad as hares when March is done.
He drove his father's four-by-four onto the baseball field,
cranked three-sixties til the ruts were deep as canyons,
deep as creases on the face of God.
Maybe others egged him on. His last indignity
was leveling a corner of the homerun fence.

The old guys standing at the mound let slip their baseball gloves,
survey the carnage on the first of May. The sky is overcast.
They look like sacks of winter-kept potatoes in their sweats.
No one understands the punks, all hepped up on Halo and designer
    drugs.
It's inconceivable that anyone would drive a truck across the infield
    grass.
Riggsy spits tobacco on the shale: *These kids — they never coulda
    played the game.*
The rest is silence deeper than when worlds burn out.
Tomorrow they will bring their hammers, nails, and rakes
to fix this greenest patch of earth before the heavens break.

Ebbets Field

Wearie Willie wipes his tears
and rests his head on Campanella's shoulder.
He can't believe the circus leaves today.

September now:
the Dodgers beat the Pirates.
There is no celebration
to mark the passing of the summer boys.

Moses and O'Malley can't agree—
where should Ebbets go?
The prophet dreams that Flushing Meadows would be nice.
O'Malley knows that once you leave the borough
Timbuktu or Tokyo are as good
as elsewhere in Noo Yawk.

Shit happened here:
Durocher cuffed a mouthy fan
somewhere in the bowels of this place;
Jackie broke down walls;
and let us not forget, in 1955,
the upset of the Yanks.

The duke sits in the empty stands.
His friends are on the plane.
Palm trees, movie stars,
Chavez Ravine,
a dynasty out west
and then the Giants leave Manhattan.

The people in the street
will not forgive O'Malley
or even say his name
without first horking on the dirty stones.

Candlestick Park, San Francisco, 1984

Exasperating place—
the San Franciscan winds

      make easy flies

impossible
                to catch.

      The ball

drops

                twenty feet away

     as Chili

throws his hands

                into the air.

Hot August night
but jacket-cold by eight o'clock.
The fans are getting restless.

Dodgers' pitcher steps up to the plate.
Just hit him in the head the guy beside me shouts
and then apologetically to me
if we wanna win that is.

Dwayne Brenna

The Big O, Montreal, 1988

How can this concrete beast be elegant?
Maybe it's the buxom lady
who shows me to my seat
or maybe it's the businessmen
who eat paté and bread
a few rows down.
(The place is almost empty
like a night café
no tango to be danced.)

Eh guy, they say, *you drink wine*?
They pour a glass—
yes, glass, not plastic cup.
I eat and drink
and listen to their lonely cheers
as Carter jacks one out:
Ooh-ooh-ooh-ooo la la!

Cleveland Stadium, circa 1990

It was a nothing game—
Cleveland and the Yanks—
far from pennant races,
not the slightest whiff
of cold October.

My dad had been an Indians' fan
since he was old enough
to listen to Herb Score:
The sun is going down,
the shadows of the lighting standards
fall across the field.

My dad, who later lost his words,
syntactic dementia.

He didn't want to go at first —
long drive round Lake Erie —
better things to do on Saturday
but when I flashed the tickets
he was sold.

We sat in Cleveland Stadium.
He was silent.
Hum of fifteen thousand fans
and still the place seemed empty.
Nothing game until the seventh;
sun went down and shadows
fell across the field.

Oh, he said, *so that's what*
Herb Score meant.
The sun went down
and made it all worthwhile.

Dwayne Brenna

Town Mead Leisure Park, Essex, 1993

Sweating out a PhD,
colonial boy
no one wants to know.

My fingers freeze in Bloomsbury;
I read sometimes with gloves on,
feet against the water pipe
underneath the desk where Marx once wrote.

Then springtime comes —
I see an ad in a magazine
BASEBALL PLAYERS WANTED
0928 7774.

In two weeks' time
we practice on a ragged cricket pitch,
horsehide wet from the incessant rain.

I've twelve new friends.
Their names don't sound like baseball names;
Their names are Phillip, Andrew, Aige.

I like them all the same
as I discard my boots
in the thatched grass of Essex,
lacing up a battered pair of cleats.

Shea Stadium, New York City, 2005

Ain't no house that Ruth built
but a tough house all the same.

Hey Pedro! Hey Martinez!
Hey dick-wad, you suck!

Guy beside me thinks I'm from New York,
I don't know why.
He turns to me and says,
That asshole's talkin trash in Shea,
his voice too loud.

An argument ensues.

The Phillies and the Mets
are playing to a nothing-nothing tie.
Sun swelters there in late July.
No one hits the ball.

Bottom of the ninth:
my wife requests a beer—
no not requests, demands—
I'm dyin here she says
(her words will live in infamy).

Now? I ask.
The bleacher boys are gone by then;
they're racing muggers to the trains.

Then I'm in the bowels of Shea,
out of sight of the playing field,
and hear the speaker *Mike Piazza coming to the plate.*

Dwayne Brenna

Concession girl says *Whaddayawant?*

A beer.

What kinda beer ya want? she asks.

Just any kind.

She pours a beer into a plastic cup.
That's seven fifty.

I shove a ten at her,
don't stay for change,
and hear the thwack of hickory,
the ground swell of an aching will to win,
the rumble rising from expensive seats down low,
and rushing through the concrete maze
I spill the beer
but don't get back in time
to see the replay on the Jumbotron,
don't even see Piazza in his homerun trot.

Which field he hit it to? I ask my wife.
Dunno, she says,
her hair dishevelled like my soul,
So parched I couldn't see.

House Made Of Pollen: Hohokam Stadium, Phoenix, 2008

At Hohokam, the pollen hangs in the air like something from
        Marquez,
    the postcard sky is dancing and awash
    in flowery ephemera.

We build our houses of this haze, thinking they'll survive
    the huffing of the Big Bad Wolf, but Hohokam knows
    that nothing lasts forever.

Old guys playing baseball don't care how much they've lost;
    they're here to play, little thinking of the pollen-burnished sun,
    how it labours on its way.

Dwayne Brenna

Cairns Field, Saskatoon, 2010

It's late; they start the game at nine o'clock.
They play two games a night
because kids love the sport. The lights are on.
I'm sitting in the stands, my arms outstretched,
my back against the cold cement. I'm smiling inwardly.
My son is playing hard like young boys should.
The infield grass is luminous, as green
as Spring in your imaginings. The lights
of Saskatoon are dots against the sky,
the deep blue sky behind right field, and there
in the cool dark night, the shining city.
Innocence itself could not shine brighter,
and I believe that no place in the world
is as joyous as this baseball field tonight.

2. Home Plate

"I don't want any doctor building a swimming pool with my knee."
— Steve Howe on knee operations

You're Gonna Like This Game

Pick-up truck brush-painted red
careening through the silent clouds of dust.
My dad is in the driver's seat,
skinny,
way too young to be a dad,
wheat chaff on the shoulders of his shirt.
He guns it up the hill;
my stomach's in my throat.
Weeee-hoooooo!
I'm sitting right beside him
staring at a baseball glove,
my brother's pancake hand-me-down.
Nicely broken in, my dad would say.
I've got my fingers crossed,
hoping I'll be good.

Then we're on the blacktop;
telephone posts go speeding by.
My dad says, *Think you're gonna like this game?*
I tell him *yeah* but I'm not sure.

We purr through town,
end up near the school,
six or seven kids already there,
swinging bats at blue belly flies.

The red door creaking open.
Don't forget your cap!
And just before it shuts
I hear my dad
Don't be shy, he says, *and tell 'em you can pitch.*

Dwayne Brenna

A Boy Looks at his Reflection in the Window

In that golden time the sun would follow him,
the birds would warble ancient hymns,
and he would hear the sermons of the stones.
In those days of wonder and delight
the boy was Mantle on his father's lawn,
watching his reflection in the window,
mimicking the Mick, his stance and stride.
On one vivacious swing the baseball bat
went twirling from his hands and through the glass.
It sounded like the loss of paradise.

Then the boy was running from the yard
to the forest where the fox hole was.
He thought he'd have to stay out there a month
but soon he heard the baying of the wolves,
the coyotes' nipping yowl, the hooting owl.
He also heard his mother calling him
and ventured to the fence's edge, the house.
His mother hugged him but his father said
You broke that window, didn't you?
The boy said no and he was sent to bed.

Next morning when the boy awoke he found
the sun was careless of him in the sky
and birds were warbling for themselves alone.

Car Ride

Always some kid's gut is doing somersaults.
He's eaten beans or onions, french fries maybe,
and you'll be sitting next to him.
The station wagon hums along,
a dozen bragging, brawling, braying boys,
rag-tag in their dirty uniforms.
Quietly he'll fart, a no-man's land of gas
and Mister Archer's windows won't roll down.
It sneaks up like an angry housecat
stalking, hissing, irrepressible.
Your eyeballs turn to marble; hold your nose,
the stench is like an earwig in your brain.
    Mister Archer hits the brakes and we pile out,
    red-eyed pigeons looking for a place to roost.

Cheats

Game of little cheats
like corking bats or greasing up the ball
or yelling *Mine!* when popping up to short.

I asked my Aussie friend
if there were cheats like that in cricket.
Dwyne, he said, *crickit is a gintleman's gyme.*

No gentleman's game this,
a sport whose teeth were cut in alleys and on stoops,
a wily, black-eyed way of making up the rules as you go,
a farmboy's swollen knuckles
or an Irish brawling game just off the street,
big-shouldered and tobacco in your eye.

I learned to cheat when I was twelve:
trapped ball but looking like a snag.
The other coach was angry.
Did you make the catch?

I nodded yes.

Afterwards my dad, his arm around me,
said, *The umpire calls the game, not you.*

Beer Gardens

Got a couple hours to kill because
we lost to Watson six to five
and me and Gary standing by the tent.
Early in the afternoon, and both of us
fourteen but taller than our moms at least.
We peer into the close and holy dark.
Inside the tent, with Camels in their sleeves,
the burly men are cradling brown glass,
their voices like the hum of Fords and Dodges.
You stay put, says Gary, *I'll get the beer.*
The sun is higher than it's ever been.
It hurts my head, a migraine coming on.
    We drink our Pilsner in the tall wild grass,
    squinting at the ladies' softball game.

Dwayne Brenna

Alger

We didn't have the words to say just what it was.
The kindest word we used was *slow*.
Alger's slow, we said, *the lights are on but no one's home*.
He should have had more brains; his head was big,
pug nose and two small eyes, his hair was shaven close.
He walked bent over like he hoped to find ten dollar bills
under every blade of grass or maybe he was swearing
at the sand beneath his running shoes.

That spring we shagged pop flies on soggy grass,
our lazy strides were mirrors of the ball's soft arc.
Alger sitting on the front steps of the school watching us.
Youse kids! Hey, youse kids! he rasped. *Say can Alga play?*
We shouted something back, likely something rude,
saw him step towards us through the mines the gophers laid.
Each uneven tuft of grass was ice to him.
Coach met him at the fence and told him *No
but you can be the bat boy if you want.*

After that, he sat with us on wooden two-by-twelves
in every town from Lake Lenore to Smuts
shrieking things like *Wumble guys! Let's wumble!*
We rubbed his bristled head for luck.
Even umpires stopped the game
while Alger did his ice-walk to the bat,
cussing at the ground with every step.
That season we went twenty-one and three.

But kids are kids, I guess, we started teasing Alger that next year,
mimicked how he walked and how he picked up bats.
One time I turned to him and said, *Let's wumble, Alga.*
He didn't move, just sat there cursing at the ground.
Didn't have much language either, but he had enough.
Scwew you Dewey, just go scwew y'self, he said.
I guess I did go screw myself that day.
Couldn't catch a routine fly to save my life.

Apology (Or Close As It Gets)

Early in the year and we've just lost again
bad. We're kneeling on the outfield grass
like witches in a sacrifice.

And I'm still fuming at the Coach.
He sent me in from third.
The catcher had the ball
when I was only half-way down the line.

The Coach is standing there
recounting all our errors:
Jimmy missed the cut-off in the second,
E-Dawg didn't get the jump,
and one too many change-ups thrown waist-high.
Oh yeah Coach says *and then there's me*
for sending Dewey in from third.

I'm looking at the grass
for errant earthworms.

Whattaya think? he barks
Just because I'm Coach
I ain't allowed to make mistakes?

Sports Day

A girl in blue jeans sitting in the stands.
My old man's car is parked along the field.
I'm spitting sunflower seeds and laughing:
someone grabbed old Pepe by the balls.
The bread smells homey in the booth
and sharp as blades the wiener on the bun.
My best friend's face a palette for Van Gogh
of mustard, ketchup, sugar, dust, and grass.
A solid thwack, it's like no other sound.
Approving murmur of old men
and some old lady cackles in the heat.
   The dust is hanging in the air at night,
     the taste of dust still lingers in my mouth.

No Fun

Never let the other team have too much fun.
Don't know who said it but it's true.

One time, against the Braves,
we walked this guy intentionally
every time we saw him at the plate.
He didn't have much fun that day.

We knew that he could hit the ball;
six taters in four games the week before.

His last at-bat
the guy stands at the wrong side of the plate,
daring us to pitch to him.

Smoky throws the first pitch
on the black.
The ump calls *Strike*!

We're pitching to him now.
The guy can't cross the plate,
not in the same at-bat
(if you'd read the rules, you'd know).
Two more fastballs down the middle
and he was shown a seat.

He didn't have much fun that day.

Bunt Defence

I'm talkin game on the line:
bottom of the ninth
and knotted up at five,
bases loaded, no one out.
I'm talkin championship,
what makes a winning side.

You know the bunt is on.
You'd do it too,
squeeze the runner home
and take the win
all the way to Stanley's pub.

The batter squares,
the runners go,
third baseman breaks for home,
so does Stretch,
the pitcher charges too.
Second goes to first
and short to third
and who's on second?
Abbot or Costello — no — get this
the guy from centre field.
Pitcher flips it to the plate,
catcher throws to first
and after that we'll see
who's buying beers at Stan's.

Voodoo

Maybe it was going overboard
to sacrifice that chicken at the game.
We do resort to voodoo
when the baseball gods aren't kind.

Couldn't even lose right.
Last game of the tournament
out came the rubber chicken,
pissed off without his feathers,
been roosting in the ball bag
since that hitless streak last spring.

Petey lit a quackgrass smudge
and shouted out some gibberish
Ooga booga booga loo.
A few of us sang *Kumbaya,*
danced a hip-hop baseball jig,
rubbed our barren bats against
that chicken's shiny ass.

Only Layton wasn't pleased.
He wouldn't say *horse shit*
if it was spilling out his mouth.
That's sacrilege plain and simple, boys.
It won't do no good.

He changed his tune, though,
when I doubled up the gap
and Sudsy hit the scoreboard out in left.
There weren't no atheists
sitting in the dugouts after that.

Next inning Layton sidled up
and asked that chicken's blessing
on his pine-tarred bat.
Not that it did him any good—
even rubber chickens
like their parish undivided.

Evening of the Tournament

Petey's setting up the tent.
I'm trying to light a fire.
Sudsy's wrapping hocks in foil,
his secret recipe,
hocks and ketchup, just a dash of coriander.
Lovingly he sets them on the grill.

It starts to rain.

We're crouched like hobos under canvas,
watching as the fire wilts,

and Sudsy gets a bright idea.
Twilight room's three blocks away.

The lead-lined clouds roll in.
The sky yawns rudely,
walls inside the tent perspire.

Later in the pub, we're drinking beer and
eating pickled eggs and chips—
they just don't hit the spot.
Some baseball player's singing karaoke;
Duke of Earl is all he knows.

It's midnight now.
We're walking to the soggy tent,
a starry sky above.
Hey, it isn't raining anymore, I say,
as if it's poured for forty days and nights.

The firebox is spitting embers
as we near the camp;
hocks are sizzling in the foil.
Some fires are harder to put out than others,
just like love or friendship —
coals are dampened but they burn within.

Our stubby fingers part the foil gingerly,
the smell of roasted coriander,
the taste of slow-cooked hocks and beans.

Fan

Five solid feet of mid-life crisis,
tired of cheating husbands, lazy kids.
She always wore a lime-green baseball hat
and sat where we could see her
in the bleachers right behind the plate.

We gauged our play by Nettie's jaundiced stare.
When the lucky breezes blew our way
she'd crack a thermos and relax,
hot black coffee scalding as her wit.
If they went the other way she soured
like a can of rotting corn.

She rode me like a borrowed donkey once.
The ump had called me out on strikes
and then I heard her softly in my ear
Hey Brenna that's a great at-bat.
Her anger mounted through the game
until it seemed that I could do no right;
an easy double play I booted in the ninth
and heard her like a harpooned seal
or sandpaper on wood.
Attaboy, Brenna, show 'em how it's done.

Canadian Oldtimers' Championship, Red Deer, 2007

Don't know why I did it.
Guess I don't like losing.

Sharp hit ball:
me charging like an aged rhino
breaking up the double play.

It's true I slid off second base
and nailed the shortstop hard,
him yawing over me
the Hindenberg plummeting to earth,

except he lived
and so did I.

Obligatory clearing of the bench
(or close to that as old time baseball gets);
threats and pointed fingers—
Manitoba coach's face so red,
looks like he fell into a barbeque.
Next time bud we're throwin at yer head.

And limping off the field,
I turn and say
What is this—ball or pussy ball?

Don't know what got into me.
Horsehide brings out things
even I don't understand.

Didn't Look That Awkward

Didn't look that awkward
coming off the mound;
his foot hit wrong.
I heard a snap
and he went tumbling
tumbling down like bricks.

It wasn't pretty.

I got to him first
and saw him clutching at his leg.
Your knee again?
He moved his lips.
No words came out.
And bending closer, looked him in the eye,
Just tell me what it is.
His face was stern as winter days.
He moved his lips again
and whispered almost audibly.

He paused to catch his breath
and then he voiced the word,
sounding like a devil
from the seventh ring of Hell:
Ambulance.

To Mrs. Towny Townsend
Chesapeake, Virginia

    Please send me fifty of
    your husband's batting disks.
    I understand you keep them
    in the back of your garage
    and that they're little more
    than painted Cool-Whip lids,
    thrown like frisbees in the gym.
    They curve and dip around the bat.

    I've heard the story many times,
    how Towny sat up in his bed
    dying of cancer at fifty-four
    and channel surfing, all his proteges
    Cuddyer, Wright, and B.J Upton
    playing on that day.
    He called his son into the room
    and spoke as best he could,
    half his larynx gone,
    Doesn't get better than this.

    I'd buy the disks
    just to be part of that story.

Blue Team

I used to think of umpires as stray dogs
with no allegiance or morality;
pretend you're friends but bite you in the ass.
They're always there to call you out on strikes
or toss you from the game, and always
with such joie de vivre, you gotta believe
they're cynical, vindictive sons-of-bitches.

I pitched against the Tigers one June night.
After it was done, the Ump stayed back
and said, *Let's see that go-to pitch again.*
He grabbed a bat, and Pete came out and caught.
We must have thrown him fifty balls. He swung
and missed with such abandon and such glee
I saw, at last, how much he loved the game.

That's how I learned to put some faith in umps,
Not trust them totally perhaps. Stray dogs
are always strays, no matter how they bark.

Funeral

We mourn his passing — Old Man Foushe was coach
and umpire in this town for thirty years.
Always old to us, I guess, his voice was
fashioned out of beer and cigarettes.
Steeee! he growled and *Baaawwrr!* and sometimes *Faauooooh!*
Embroidered freely on the diamond game
and made us think that we were in the bigs.
The fingers on his left hand bitten off;
run-in with an angry swather blade.
He couldn't count both strikes and balls at once.
Stood there mostly like an ancient buffalo
but got excited by a hit, a play at home.
    We hoist him on our shoulders like we never did,
    his casket seeming lighter than he was.

Double Play

Ball hit sharply.
Shortstop makes the play
and charging in
straight route to the ball —
a lesson in efficiency —
gathers it like a robin's egg
in his soft hands.
He tosses to

the second baseman,
straddling the bag,
barehands, leaps —
a ballet of his own —
a diamond Baryshnikov
and throws mid-air
above the sliding runner.

On first, the baseman scissors.
Horsehide slaps cowhide
one eyeblink before
the runner reaches.

Umpire's hand shoots out;
loves to be part of a pretty play.

Ya Gotta Want the Ball

Coaching in the little leagues
I tell 'em, *Boys, you gotta want the ball.*

City playdowns,
bottom of the sixth, and we're in tight.

Jimmy's playing third,
was in the outfield almost all the game;
he's shaking like a dashboard hula girl.

I call time out and bring the boys together.
What you thinkin, Jimmy?

I'm thinkin I don't want the ball, he says.

I turn to my first baseman.
What you thinkin, Stretch?

I'm thinkin it'd shore be nice, he drawls,
if Jimmy doesn't get the ball.

Umpiring

Shoulder's blown,
the knees gave out —
ain't nothin left
but join the blue team
after all.

I'm first-base ump in Triple A:
the runner beats the throw
and breaks down past the bag,
outside the line but turning in.

The baseman tags him
but I call the runner safe
because he didn't
make a move for second.

Better eyes on a potato,
the head coach shouts.
His crony calls me *homey*.

I tell em *Read the rules.*

Next runner's out by seven steps
but when I make the call
the coach pipes up again
You sure he isn't safe?

Coaching Clinic

In just-spring
the dirty snow is packed
like ancient hoodoos on the curbs,
frozen and then melted
and then frozen again.
No way to keep my car clean
in the pocked streets.

On Saturdays we sit and listen,
Iorg or Fanning holding forth,
easy in our plastic chairs
in some backroom in some hotel,
baseball in the sweetness of the air
we haven't dared to breathe
since last November,
in the wakened cadence of old men
the pale pink haze above the town.

WinnWell

Perhaps he stood like Jesse James
in the shadows of the parking lot at Cairns,
thirteen and thievery was still romance,
his cap at the impertinent angle of hip-hop.
For him, my father's baseball glove was candy,
in a moment tasted and then gone;
with wrench or hammer busted
out the window of my car,
retreated to a pawnshop with his prize.
What was it worth? Five dollars, maybe ten?

My father's catcher's mitt was all I had of him
except his eyes, his voice, his way of standing —
old WinnWell, the kind that Elston Howard used,
pancaked, with a blackened eye.
He had to drive to Saskatoon to find a mitt
like that in 1961, built for the right hand.
More than any man I ever knew, he loved
the taste of competition and the win.
When fathers die, you lose
a little more of them each day.
Now I've lost the smell of leather
and the oil he used,
his hand print in the glove.

3. Hard Ball

"Blind people come to the park just to listen to him pitch."
— Reggie Jackson on Tom Seaver

Fastball

You see in living colour after that.
Pure white smoke
and bee bee at the knees;
arrives like a punch in the face
or a pail of cold water
and hops and sometimes drops
and sometimes disappears
(ask any ump)
and thwack goes the mitt.
A Foley artist couldn't make that sound.

Sniper fire
from the un-grassy knoll;
statement of unbending bluntness,
black and white
and no détente;
you on that side,
me on this,
and hit it if you can.

Chatter

Hum hum hummunuh
  hey righty hey right side
    hey boss hey li'l rider.

Show him the dark one now
  show him a seat
    show him a seat right hander.

Quality pitch right here
  a bee bee at the knees
    dis guy's a looker babe.

No free rides now
  got the stick glued to his shoulder
    fastball down the middle hummunuh.

Touch some black now sugar
  hey you hey you hum
    throw him sumpin he ain't seen.

Long strike that counts fer you
  go after him push rock arm
    throw him the dirty li'l wrinkle.

Throw him the nasty li'l pill
  pull the string now hummer
    show him da back door curve.

That don't hurt sweet daddy
  first was open anyway big arm
    go get the next guy hummunuh.

Curveball

I ain't no scientist
but still I know a curve ball when I see one.

Some physicist once set out
to plot the wind resistance
on a baseball's seams.
He declared, in writing,
the curve's impossibility,
an illusory state:
The curve ball doesn't really curve,
he said.

Did he ever play the game?

And how does he account
for this illusion:
some balls curve six inches
others curve three feet?

Tell Frank Viola that his curve ball doesn't curve
the next one's at your head.

It's like deciding that the world is flat.
Climb Mount Olympus first,
then tell me that.

Knuckleball

Crazy pitch
thrown from the knuckles or the fingertips
but easy on the wrist.

> Who invented this madness?
> Wilhelm? Niekro?
> Even the names don't scan.

The catchers' bane;
they use a mitt
as big as all outdoors.

> It dances like a Broadway chorus girl,
> step ball change
> then off to New York.

It quivers
like a new lover
at first touch.

> *There are two theories*
> *on hitting knuckleballs*
> said Charlie Lau

Neither of them works.

Split Finger

Used to throw the screwball
but pronated hands and elbows
don't make healthy arms.
Fernando Valenzuela found this out
too late.

Took a while
to stretch my fingers out
but I jammed in the ball
and held it there for weeks,
watching Jen on TSN.

Then winter came.
I threw it in the gym
for six months straight.

So what's it do?
It fades
like memories of Mathewson.
It dies
like a wounded skunk,
leaves an odour at your door.

When it's working
no one hits that thang.

Circle Change

Kitten staring at a bowl of milk;
husband at his newly wedded wife;
both of these are you or Pavlov's dog.
The bell will make you salivate;
so too the floating beach ball coming at you
      slowly
            slowly
                  slowly.
The sun itself could not burn more bright.
You might swing your bat and knock it round
the edges of the earth, like vikings in a Python sketch.
You're falling into outer space, black holes,
sun falls from the sky and you swing at
      nothing
            nothing
                  nothing.

Catcher

Broken knuckles
and arthritic knees.
Wears the tools of ignorance
as they say.

Moves like a pensioner
at thirty-two.
Shoulder broke in three —
collision
at the plate.

Some call it ignorance.
Really it's just love
of brawling, busting up,
everything that's tough.
It makes him feel alive.

Base

A lowly being, unsophisticated, bestial
suspiciously born and bred;
or else a place where one is safe,
a sanctuary
defensible by soldiers;
or else a square of canvas, plastic, leatherette,
twelve inches by twelve inches.

                        Ball

            Buffet, dancing, midnight copulation
            celebration and festivity;
            or else a gland where sperm is made
            sometimes called the testes;
            or else an object round and hard,
            eighty-eight inches of red waxed thread
            in overlapping stitches.

Seams/Seems

Seems like a good place to begin,
the fault lines of the globe,
centrifugal force and gravity
keeping it together.

Everything you need to know
in the twisting of those seams;
they might be lucky horseshoes
or one unbroken line.

Red dot by day,
curve's coming your way.
Ball white and bright,
fastball in flight.

The ancient humming of the earth
needs to be heard as well
before the grass is blighted
and the blood red sand is burnt.

Dwayne Brenna

The Origins of Baseball

Pundits crow and sports announcers speak
of how dear Abner thought up this here game,
how Al Spalding happened to be there.
Stitched and ready was the five ounce orb,
the grass already manicured in Boston and New York.

But even unread schoolboys know
that baseball was invented in Saskatchewan
when Henry Kelsey found the perfect stone,
not regulation weight perhaps and without seams,
rounded by the centuries of ice
and polished in the river that the glaciers left.

The big man threw his heater to a brave
whose name was unpronounceable
and not preserved in record books.
There were no playing fields of course
and so they set up bases in the fort,
cheap seats in the ramparts where the women watched.

A gorgeous fetlock of an elk became the bat
and with that implement, a factor of the Hudson's Bay
was first to conquer the short porch in right;
he touched all four as friendly drums
were sounding out the box score far across the plain.

The Tao of Baseball

But for what you think
the tidy orb will find its proper path.
Welcome nothing, nothing to expect.

Mind like a mirror:
no worries and no fears,
accepting like the hunchback
what life throws at you.

If your hand's a chicken, lay an egg.
If a bow, then shoot.
Hunchbacks do what hunchbacks do,
beg along the silken road.

Not I
not me
the universal all
one with the Game
its subtle dance:

the pitcher leads,
the batter follows,
and the umpire calls.

All must be forgiven,
all must be forgotten,
a lousy memory's best.

I see you standing like a wooden rooster.

Gets late early out here
Yogi said.
The game is long.

*Cut my pizza in six slices,
can't eat twelve.*

Eat the wind and drink the dew.

Dance,
breathe,
fall in love,
make sushi.

Why are the Japanese
so good at this game?

4. The Mound of Venus

"I'd rather hit than have sex."
— Reggie Jackson

Ladies' Softball

It isn't right. She throws just like a man.
Stands looking in — a sigh — a toss of mane
and then a flurry, legs, long fingers, arms
unleash a dazzled whisper in your ear.
Her eyes are soft, forgiving as a church.
There is no hint of savagery.
She could be thrumming on an autoharp
or in the glistening act of making love.
In my dreams, she can't resist and takes me
by the hand and leads me to her bed,
Last Picture Show still playing in my head,
teacher's wife and schoolboy found in an embrace.
   I sit and watch the softball game, my mind
   awash and lost on shipwrecked seas with her.

How to Talk to Girls

My baseball buddy's getting a divorce
and looking like a ragged crop of oats.

He asks me how to talk to girls
and where to find them.

Dunno, I say, *a church maybe,
a supermarket's good.*

So tell me what to say to them.

Whatever worked when you were twenty-one.

I can't remember back that far, he says.

I look toward the lowering sky
*Go into a grocery store and find the nearest lady,
ask her where the frozen raccoon is.*

The game's in Hudson Bay that week.
We stop for Gatorade and oranges.
Cashier's pretty as a well-turned double play.
My buddy is appreciative.
Where's the frozen raccoon kept? he asks.

She's cool, this country girl,
she doesn't drop the ball.
Prob'ly in the freezer at the back.

Afterwards we're sitting in the car,
my buddy sad and spitting doggie doo.
Your line about the raccoon doesn't work, he moans.

I tell him, *No, it works.*
The problem is, ya gotta find a town
where frozen raccoon isn't on the menu.

Fat Girls in Yorkton

Fat lady struggles through the door,
walker jerking her along.
It's hard to tell her age —
sixty-five or seventy —
been heavy all her life, I guess,
two fat daughters at her flanks.
Her arms have jowls.

I'm paying for my l'il cowpoke breakfast.
Nine o'clock on Sunday,
game's at ten.
My buddy's flirting with the girl at the till;
they like a man in uniform
(even a baseball uniform).

Fat lady trips on a ragged carpet edge,
walker leaps on its hind legs
and then she's like a skyscraper,
demolition charge laid at the base.
Knee buckles underneath the cellulite
and down, down, down she goes,
one storey atop the next.

Fat lady topples, spirals, falls,
her hands a drowning woman's
frantic for my shoulders, neck.
We sink together to the carpet
and then I'm splayed beneath her,
noses almost touching —
a thing Fellini might have dreamed.

The daughters are embarrassed;
they look to see who's watching.
Other patrons go about their business,
stepping gingerly around us.
Does this happen every day in Yorkton?

Fat lady whispers, *I'm sorry about this*
almost in a lover's tone.
I whisper back, *Don't worry*
I'll get you on your feet.
She moans in a girlish way.
It takes a man and a half to get me up.

Not sure where to put my hands
I try to lift.
She weighs about four hundred pounds.
My buddy grins as if he's caught us in a motel room.
You havin fun? he asks.

This ain't no time for jokes.

A man beneath a burning car,
I push.
At last, she's standing upright, leaning on her walker
shaken, out of breath.

We'll take you back to the home now, mom,
daughter's narrow voice.
Her gaze is stern
as though she's caught me
buggering her mother on the table by the window.

Give her a break, I say
but only to myself
She's maybe longed for waffles all this week.

I watch as the van she's riding in
edges off the parking lot,
her broad face turned toward me,
leper going back to quarantine.

Physiotherapy

Good thing I've never made a cent
playing this game
or I'd be sad,
career-ending injury and all.

Happened like this:
passed ball,
shale was wet behind the plate.
I'm running to the screen,
one foot this way
the other that,
then lying on the ground
my testicles in hand,
whispering expletives to the laden sky.

Doc said it coulda been worse,
coulda been a hernia.
As it is, my nuts are black
as Turkish coffee.
It aches when I get a woody.

So now I'm in therapy—
physiotherapy—
which is the upside of pain.
I got this therapist,
she's twenty-three.
I'm on my back
three times a week.
She puts my foot on her shoulder
and rubs my area.
Breaking down the scars, she says.
Oh yes, got scars I haven't even mentioned.

Where does it hurt today, Joe?
Anywhere you touch me, baby.

Lonely Hearts

Slender, young, romantic, thoughtful —
that describes my brother.
If you'd rather spend an afternoon
with chubby end-stage alcoholic male,
54, in stained tee and loafers,
meet me in the parking lot at Fenway.
I'll be sitting on the tailgate of my pickup
(nineteen ninety-six blue Dodge)
barbecuing franks and swilling beer.
We can spend sweet, silent hours
admiring the lushness of the infield grass,
savouring a firm, round homer,
watching as the sun goes down
over the green monster.
Only baseball-savvy females need apply.
Box 2045

Cantankerous Baseball Card Collector Seeks Large-Breasted Statistician

If the words "Pete Rose" and "orgasm"
and "give me the remote"
are not, for you, miles apart
and if you can tell me at first sight
who was pitching to Rick Monday
when he made the Blue Jays blue that night
then let us meet at Joe's
in front of the TV.
We'll play the baseball kissing game
which Dizzy Dean made famous:
I'll kiss you on the strikes,
you kiss me on the balls.
Man, 41. My name is Sid
but never call me Sidney.
Box 5023

Groupie Wanted

You're a single female with a mischievous smile
and low self-esteem.
I'm an ex-baseball player with groupie fetish
seeking Susan Sarandon look-alike
to help perform astonishing array of sex-acts,
each involving velvet handcuffs
and an ostrich feather.
If any of this interests you,
we can meet one wintry Saturday
and live out loud
before spring training starts.
Box 6019.

Sarandon

You gotta love Sarandon, man. Any chick that can talk ol Nuke into wearing a garter belt is all right. Could teach me to breathe through my eyelids any day.

She'd be a lot of work. Don't get me wrong. She'd be a heap of work. Like you're trying to kiss her and she's going off about animal rights. Or the benefits of saw palmetto. Or the flood in New Orleans. Or the evils of George Bush. There'd always be a catch. You've finally gotten her into bed, and it's just like in White Palace. You've got those round-as-earth breasts in your hands and she whispers, "What about the child labourers in Cambodia?"

"Let's talk baseball."

"The steroid scandal?" she asks. "The 1919 Black Sox?"

"Teach me how to breathe through my eyelids."

Woody Allen

Between the clarinet and Annie Hall, he's at a baseball game beside a woman who could be your daughter. She's neither glamorous nor plain in her mix-match of fur and cotton. Two rows down, a fan in a loud shirt tells the tale of the Clipper to his meek cousin. "Never to be equaled," he crows, "forty seven straight in '43. And that was on a sore left hip." Woody frowns, squints at the glare of the stadium lights. The fan won't stop. "Then he met that ho Monroe, and everything went to rat-shit."

Currently in love with the fur-and-cotton woman, Woody needs to defend her honour, needs to defend the honour of all women. "Marilyn was nice," he half-apologizes. His spectacles begin to fog.

The guy cranes his neck. "She was a ho. She ruined the best player in the game."

"And you have that on good authority?"

"I read the papers, buddy."

"Well, Joe just happens to be sitting over there. Why don't you ask him?"

Twenty feet away, a man in a crisp suit turns gracefully to the loud-shirted fan. "I've heard your blather," he says. "Marilyn was the biggest star of this or any other age. And it was fifty-six in '41."

Woody winks at the camera. "Don't you wish life was like that?"

The Mound of Venus

Why was she so adamant
we do it on the baseball field?
After dark, she took my hand,
unfurled a woolen blanket
on the mound's raked shale.
Deft her hands and giggling;
I giggled too, I guess,
chewing juicy fruit and
jeans around my ankles,
her skin brown and pebbled.
It seemed like sacrilege,
this the place where
ancient heroes lived.

Afterwards she kissed me
with an open mouth,
a kiss that said,
You're mine now;
everything you've done
out here until this night
was but a child's dream.

Dwayne Brenna

5. Bambino and the Boys

"Hot as hell, ain't it, Prez."
— Babe Ruth to US President Harding

Autograph

The Big Bambino loved to sign his name,
not because of his calligraphy.
He thought that what he autographed was his —
scraps of paper, balls and bats,
pickup trucks and buses, candy bars.
He wouldn't sign brassieres —
it wasn't done back then —
but ladies' arms and legs and asses.
He capitalized if they wore glasses.
Trees and rivers, mountains,
once he tried to sign the earth
in letters three feet high
by pissing in the New York snow,
got all the way to Ru
and then ran out of juice.
That signature was worth a million bucks.
It melted the next day.

Pointing to the Stands

The Big Bambino points toward the stands.
He's done this many times
in other epochs, using other names —
Napoleon and Caesar
Wellington, Canute —
and others who will not be mentioned.

Some men seem to get their way:
by pointing to the stands
the ball goes there.

The Babe on Film

On film he is a cartoon of himself
barrel-chested, spindly legs.
His chubby face is not the Babe
but Baby Ruth, a chocolate confection,
too much sugar for the pancreas.
It must be staged, the camera close, impossible—
he raises eyebrows, mugs, and points to right,
clock-armed like an actor in an old-time play.
Nothing William Bendix did could be too large
for this man born of his own head.

Exit right on cue the ball as tightly wound
as Babe himself, and when he trots the bases
legs move double time, sixteen feet per second.
Now they show the film at twenty-four.
The Babe is packaged like a candy bar
good and evil simple in the grainy black-and-white,
but where's the man who drinks and smokes and swears,
where's the boy who needs to be reformed?

The House that Ruth Built

He built this palace with his bulky arms,
each golden swing a nail driven home.
The grass was watered with his sweat,
the sunshine was his glittering eye
(on days when he was not hung over).

I hear he was a Broadway kind-of-guy.
Boston was too small for him.
He loved the ladies and the jack.
The President had less of both.
He didn't have as good a year as me.

Guys like Gehrig wouldn't understand,
his statue at the home run fence,
but Babe could maybe tell you why
they're tearing down his house today.

Footnote[1]

And what of poor old Wally Pipp,
his life a cautionary tale?
Never ask for aspirin in the dressing room.
Gehrig might be waiting in the wings
to never miss a game for fifteen years
until a rare disease would strike him down.
That's the stuff that movies are made of,
the Yankee Clipper and the Iron Man.

Okay, it wasn't quite like that.
Wally didn't have a headache.
Huggins benched him, that was all.
Without Ruth the Yanks were floundering.
Something needed to be done.
Who remembers Wally's infield glories,
how he went to Cincinatti that next year,
hit .291 and led the team in RBI's?

What must it be like to be a footnote
in the legend of another man,
relegated to a ring of silent hell
where no one wants to hear your side?
Wally never once complained.
He came back to New York on Veteran's Day.
There were no movies made about his life,
just the ones he showed in his own head.

---

1   Walter Clement Pipp (February 17, 1893 – January 11, 1965) was an American first baseman in Major League Baseball, now best remembered as the man who lost his starting role to Lou Gehrig at the beginning of Gehrig's streak of 2,130 consecutive games. (Wikipedia)

Dwayne Brenna

Christy

Because his mother led the choir
he wouldn't play on Sundays,
take a drink or gamble with the boys.
Married to one woman all his life.
Made men shiver with his fade-away.
How he got McGraw to love him
no one ever knew.

A play at home and Christy slid.
Umpire asked him *Were you out or safe?*
He wouldn't tell a lie,
not for the wide wide world of sports.
I was out, he said, recumbent in the sand.
It was a game then, after all.

Mickey and the Stripper

Sally knew who Mantle was,
Oklahoma's answer to DiMaggio.
She offered him a private dance,
took him all the way around the world,
stopped for crepe suzettes in France,
in Singapore he caught a nasty grippe.
His eyes were black as bitumin
when he left her bed at 6 am,
late for curfew since they played at one —
lucky thing that Billy had his back.

At noon, she woke up smiling,
phoned her bookie, bet against the Yanks
double what she'd earned the night before.
There ain't nobody hits a baseball
after Sally's given him the works.
She hears the broadcast on her radio.
Mick is shiny as a silver coin.
Musta pored some ice cubes in his jock;
four for five with two home runs,
makes a circus catch in centre field.
That's how Sally said she learned
that Oklahomans are like pickaxes,
harder than the rocks they mine.

Dwayne Brenna

1951 — Some Photographs
   (based on Jane Leavy's biography of Mickey Mantle)

Now the time of hit and myth, the centuries collide
as click the camera shudders at the waste of youth
and primal fathers go not gentle to the sacrifice.
The Mick had always said he'd take Joe's place.

Nineteen and a surfer boy's good looks — surfing
down the Oklahoma chat — *The kid's a rockhead*
that's how Joe described him to the press, but Stengel says
There ain't no white kid faster, home to first.

Here's a grainy photograph: shadows fall in 1951,
Mantle's charging for the ball as Joe calls out
That patch of grass is mine til I retire.
Blind Tiresias could see that it was Mickey's ball.

Happened once or twice before—the groundsmen didn't
     leave
the metal cap in place, the drainpipe begging for an injury
tangles Mick's old high school cleats, the vomit-making
angle of his leg still painful after sixty years.

The Yankee Clipper basket-catches in another shot.
The kid lies face down near the indentation in the grass,
his right big toe is pointing to the angry gods.
Enter now the chorus with their dismal song.

Mickey's handsome face is buried in the grass, too much hurt
to look at, Joe is kneeling by the frightened kid
Just lie still — they're comin for you now.
It was the only time all season that Joe spoke to him.

Another shot and first out of the bullpen Houk, Silvera
didn't get their picture taken much that year, except for this.
Seemed to take forever til the stretcher came.
Almost like a funeral, Mickey's carted to the dressing room.

One last photo on the gurney: Mickey looking down in
    disbelief.
He'll never look that young again, the right leg seems
no longer his; the trainer is concerned, but even Oedipus
must first put needles in his eyes before the holocaust's
    complete.

Symmetry

Three,
the trinity
Maris, Mantle, Ford;
three strikes, three outs

and multiples of three,
nine batsmen and nine innings,
sixty feet six inches to the mound,
between the bases ninety feet.

What comes in threes?
Accidents, good luck,
a clown's routine,
a song's refrain,
sometimes kittens,
sometimes pups,
third wheels,
a three-run homer,
and Divinity.

Casey

Casey hunkers down behind a desk in Oakland,
gives a loan to anyone who asks.
They got these flower children here, he says
Who knows if you should water 'em or plant 'em?
He quit the Mets too soon.
There comes a time and I've had plenty of 'em.
Bugs him now that Seaver
has commenced to being wonderful.
I'll never make the same mistake of gettin' old again.

Stats and the Great Players

The last to hit .400,
fifty-six straight games,
seven hundred fourteen homers,
sixty-one in sixty-one
(asterisk after that).

Stats don't tell the story,
not all of it at least.

How was the pitching back in '41
when Williams hit .400?
How many times did scorers turn an error to a hit
when Joltin Joe was streaking past Wee Willie?
What were the baseballs like
Ruth pounded from the park?
And what did Maris face,
what devils sick of sin,
with blotchy skin, his hair torn out in clumps?

We are not numbers or geometry;
the essence of our struggle
doesn't square.

Drysdale

You won't know him by his playing card
just his squinting eyes, laconic grin.
Those eyes could burn down houses made of brick.
That grin could make the devil hide his face.
You might see his windup on the internet,
his motion a slow drawl, with elbows upside down
like pterodactyl wings. You might even see
the batsman dive for cover, twice in one at-bat.

Some pitchers have a special DNA
that turns them into bastards in the field.
Gibson had it. So did Marichal, McLain.
But no one had it more than Drysdale.
Oh sure, he could be affable as hell;
he'd bean you and then ask to sign the bruise.

Step into the batter's box and meet the man.
He sees you digging in—that's a mistake
but everyone's a hero once, until they learn.
He sees your proud back foot and grins.
That windup, like a dentist telling you relax.
His side-arm throw is coming from the wrong side
of third base, and hit the dirt, my friend.

If you're lucky, he'll forget to put you in his book
of mother-fuckers needing to be beaned.

Dwayne Brenna

Scully
> **(Vin Scully is the longstanding play-by-play announcer for the Los Angeles Dodgers.)**

What he says
is etched in scrolls and tablets,
every thought a sentence
mimicking the languor of the game.
Wilson makes the throw
and pulls Clark
down the right field line.
The throw was rushed.
He didn't have to rush the throw.
He's skittery,
skittery,
he rushed the throw.

His voice
the reedy song of geese
and autumn breeze through cattails,
voice of trees and rivers,
hunting days and fishing,
makes you want to build a boat.

Forty days and forty nights
and then you hear that voice
Skittery,
that's what David was.
In the end he slew Goliath
with a stone.

Baseball's Music

Perhaps a gaudy oldster with bony hands
in well-pinned baseball cap and leisure suit
crouches at his wheezing instrument
madly fusing Karloff and Babe Ruth.
Maybe it's the squawk and roll of trumpets,
flyby of the murderous toothpaste tubes;
an upright sergeant sings *God Bless America*
as we salute the living and the dead.
Or it's Satchel in his swell fedora
smiling handsome as he tink-tink-tinkles
Waller, Joplin, Jelly Roll, and Artie Shaw
'Taint nobody's business if they do.
    But I say baseball's music is the kid
    who plays his mouth harp lonely on the bus.

Dwayne Brenna

Wonderboy
        (based on Bernard Malamud's *The Natural*)

The oak was felled by lightning
and lightning still in the wood
submitted to the lathe
and pitched like Stradivarius,
the rhythm of the grain so perfect,
the balance like a ballerina.
Felt like a toothpick in his hands.

And when at last he lifted it
and swung it earnestly
was heard a mighty resonating crack!
Its own echo echoed.

He dubbed it Wonderboy
and when he fell from grace
none else could lift the splinters,
none could hold the thing.

Ellis
    (from a story by David Halberstam)

They had to break the breast bone
to get at his heart,
six-inch scalpel wound,
the tubes are everywhere,
one taped to his nostril, another
running up the inside of his elbow.

He watches TV every day,
Boston and the Yanks and
Mama, he says, *they pay them boys
a hundred thousand dollars.*

Maybe he's delirious.

You just rest up now, Ellis, save your strength.

No, it's true, he says, *and Mama,
in a couple years them boys'll make a million.*

This is just too much.
I don't know why.

No one makes a million dollars, Ellis.

All the players' faces sunburned green.
Never thought I'd see the day
when TV came in color.

Out the window everything he sees is gray.
To think we played it just for love back then.

Interview with Jim Fanning

The interview was wonky from the start.
Tell us what you think of Ellis Valentine.
Did he keep his curfew late last week?
These are grown-up men, Jim said,
I ain't nobody's mama in this league.

Kinda overcast that day but
from the press box he could see
Ellis and the batboy warming up.
That was odd enough but Ellis
made him run on every throw.

One was in the dugout, one was in the stands,
mostly he just rolled it on the grass.
Would you look at Ellis now, Jim said,
he's messin with the batboy's head.

When they put the microphones away,
the tv man looked hard at Jim and said,
More like he's messin with himself.
Ever heard of cocaine, Jim?

Mobile, Alabama

We are the nameless ones,
we are the ageless ones.
We play down alleys sometimes,
bully boys and quickly gone.
Ya gotta be mobile in Mobile, Alabama.

Was I born in nineteen-six
or nineteen-eight? or somewhere in
betwixt? My momma couldn't tell you.
How old would you be
if ya didn't know how old you was?

Down the street, across from the big white church
some boys was hanged.
Didn't do much, didn't do nothin maybe
but they was hanged.
Some white folks said they caught 'em with a girl,
white girl had her knickers down around her knees
and so them boys was hanged.

We play with sticks and balls
in the lot behind the lumber yard,
we play until our mammas call us home.

Don't know nothin 'bout my old man.
He comes and goes,
sometimes he eats with us
but mostly he just comes home late,
the whisky on his breathe like danger.
Kicked me once so hard,
was pissin blood for seven days.

Our mamma help us,
our mamma treat us good.
This is the way the world begins
in Mobile, Alabama.

Satch's Blues

Met him on the road and I sold my soul.
I met him on the road and sold my soul.
        Stayin on the road is the Devil's toll.

It looks like Kansas if ya ain't got jack.
Yeah, it looks that way if ya got no jack.
        I'm keepin my life in a gunny sack.

No grass on the field behind third base,
Only sand in the field behind third base.
        Trouble's etched in the lines on my face.

Them boys in the bigs got their fine cigars.
Fellas in the bigs got their fine cigars.
        Never seen a bus cuz they ride in cars.

Put me in the big time just one day,
Ol Satch'd teach 'em white boys
                how to play.

Stealing Home

Jackie takes a lead.
He stutter steps and then a race
for home, with coals for eyes.

> Branch Rickey said he couldn't pick
> just any coloured man to break
> the dark dark chains apart.
> He had to be a guy
> the managers could get behind,
> not proud or sassy.
> *His people are his own worst enemy.*
> What did Rickey mean by that?

And then a race for home
as Yogi steps across the plate.
The batter doesn't even swing,
let Jackie do it by himself.
Coincidence of ball and glove and foot.
The umpire loves a pretty play,
he doesn't hesitate
and Yogi's climbing up the side of him.

> Out or safe, who knows?
> but man that Jackie moved.
> You couldn't tell
> how many generations weighed him down.

Acknowledgements

The author would like to thank his writing group — David Carpenter, Don Kerr, John Livingstone Clark, David Margoshes, and Tom Bentley Fisher — for all the feedback they provided about these poems. Special thanks to Robert Currie, who edited the book with a sure hand, and to Paul Wilson, who believed in it. A thank you to Trey Strecker, at *Nine*, who first published some of these poems. And, as always, thanks to my wife and sons for their love and support.

Mostly, though, thank you to the guys who played baseball with me all those years, who put up with my shenanigans, and who are a part of many of the stories told in this book.

"Candlestick Park," "House Made of Pollen," and "Ebbets Field" were previously published in *Nine: A Journal of Baseball History and Culture* (18, 2).

"Lonely Hearts," "Cantankerous Baseball Card Collector Seeks Large-Breasted Statistician" and "Groupie Wanted" were suggested by letters to *The London Review of Books*.

Dwayne Brenna's baseball career began in his home town of Naicam, Saskatchewan when he was five, shagging pop flies in the pasture with his older brother and his dad. As a young boy, he was part of a baseball team that lost many league championships to the dreaded Dahlton Sandlots. At the age of fifteen, he played shortstop for the Naicam Vikings Senior Men's team. He also played for teams in Regina and Saskatoon, at one time holding the Saskatoon Senior Men's League record for most innings pitched in a single season.

He has published poems and stories in various literary journals, including the *Antigonish Review*, *Nine,* and *Grain*. His radio play about Casey Stengel, *There Comes A Time in Every Man's Life (And I've Had Plenty of Them)* was broadcast on CBC Radio. He is the author of several books, including *Scenes From Canadian Plays* (Fifth House), *Eddie Gustafson's Guide To Christmas* (Coteau), and *Emrys' Dream: Greystone Theatre in Words and Photographs* (Thistledown). His most recent book, *Our Kind of Work: the Glory Days and Difficult Times of 25th Street Theatre*, was short-listed for the Non-fiction Award at the 2011 Saskatchewan Book Awards.

Brenna lives in Saskatoon with his wife Bev. When he's not teaching drama or directing plays at the University of Saskatchewan, Brenna is a utility infielder for the Riverhurst Thumpers.